T0149390

Single Parenting:
My Child and I

Adauzo Ijeoma Ubah

AuthorHouse™ UK Ltd.
500 Avebury Boulevard
Central Milton Keynes, MK9 2BE
www.authorhouse.co.uk
Phone: 08001974150

Published by AuthorHouse 2/10/2012

ISBN: 978-1-4678-8231-6 (sc)
ISBN: 978-1-4678-8232-3 (e)

Unless otherwise indicated all scripture quotations is taken
from The Holy Bible, New International Version®
Copyright © 1973, 1978, 1984 by International Bible Society.
Used by permission of International Bible Society.

DEDICATION.

This book is specially dedicated to all single parents and children from single parent home.

Table of Contents

1. Single Parenting – An Introduction.

Single parenting means one adult either man or woman raising a child or children alone without the assistance of another adult at home.

Single Parenthood.

/\

Choice (voluntary).   Chance (involuntary).

↓   ↓

Adoption.   Desertion.

Surrogacy.   Widowhood.

Marriage break-up.   Teenage pregnancy.

Distant marriage.

|

Choice/Chance.

↓

Adoption.

Marriage break-up.

Desertion.

The accurate language to use for people raising children alone and people raising children with their partner has been a controversial issue especially in research. The languages used in describing different families vary, for single parents, we have 'sole-parent', 'lone-mother', 'lone-father'; 'absent-parent' used for the parent that is not with the children; 'custodian-parents' used for the parent in custody of the children 'non-resident father' used for the father that is not living with the family; 'co-parent' and 'intact-home' used for home with both biological parents living together; 'non-custodian parent' used for the parent that is not in custody of the children; 'in and out parent' and 'near and far parent' are also used for separated couple; 'motherless family' used for families without the mother; 'fatherless family' used for families without father; 'shared-parenting' used for separated or divorced couple that their children spend a particular time with the parent they are not living with as agreed by both couple; 'blended family' used for family that consists both biological and step children of one or both couple living together.

Single parenthood is wide in the sense that there are circumstances that are not by choice that can lead to single parenting. Single parents are always seen in the negative side but the issue is that circumstances beyond someone's control can lead to it. Single parenting can be by choice or by chance. An example of single parenthood by choice is divorce and adoption where a woman decides not to marry and adopt one or more children. An example of single parenthood by chance is widowhood. Widowhood is something no normal person will pray for but once it comes, the person has to bear the load of two alone. Another example of single parenting by chance is desertion in which a woman is pregnant in a marriage/

relationship and the man runs away from home without the awareness of the woman or they already have children and the man runs away from home. Some other category of single parenting may fall on either choice or chance. An example of single parenthood that could be by choice or chance is adoption. A woman may decide not to get married because of one reason or the other and adopt a child or children. This is single parenthood by choice. A woman who is no longer getting younger and nobody is asking her hand in marriage may decide to adopt. When such woman needs company and no man wants to marry her and she has the resources to adopt, she may decide to do so. This is single parenthood by chance. It is her situation and not choice that makes her to do so. Whether single parenthood is by choice or chance, the issue is that one person is doing what two people are supposed to do together. Most times, it is the woman that is the single parent. Home of single father exists especially in the case of widowhood but it is minimal.

It is an obvious fact that raising children alone is not an easy task. It is said that two heads are better than one. In the family, the role of the man at home varies from the role of the woman at home. When a woman takes up the responsibility of both the man and her, it is tasking and vice versa. In trying to be both man and woman of the family, it will of course cause stress which directly or indirectly affects the children and the parent. Despite the fact that finance may not be the issue in this case, the type of parenting will always tell on the children that are being raised alone if not properly handled. For this reason, this book is aimed at helping single parents manage stress and raise their children in a way that they will not differ with the both parent children.

2. Kinds of Single Parenting.

a. Teenage Pregnancy.

Definition:

Teenage pregnancy is a young girl being pregnant outside marriage. Teenage age varies in different countries; it could be age within 18, 16, or 12 years old.

Causes:

1. Search for father – figure: Search for affection, appreciation and true love. This comes especially from children from broken home, adopted and foster child that does not receive enough love and care, and children that do not get love and care from either parent. These girls go out of their way to seek for love from someone who seems to be like a father. In the course of this search for father-figure they may fall into the wrong hand that will abuse them sexually. Some girls also seek father-figure because their father is not always at home. Modern day adults are too career-conscious that they do not provide the basic responsibility at home which is love and care. Children

wake up and go to bed without setting their eyes on their parents except for weekends. On weekends, the parents may not have enough time to spend with the child due to one programme or the other to catch up with.

2. Lack of sexuality education: Sexuality education is very important for children and it must start from childhood. Some parents have the wrong impression that if they give their child sexuality education, they will be spoilt but the reverse is the case. Parents should start by telling their child parts of their body without skipping any of them. Some parents will start from hair to toe but call the penis and vagina private parts. When you call them private parts, the child will like to know what makes that part private. In the course of enquires and exploitation, the child may fall a victim of teenage pregnancy. As the child is about to get to teenage age, you inform her of the menstruation, how she can take care of herself at that time. Tell her about all the cycle in a woman including ovulation and free period. You need to be honest with her so that she can trust you. Sexuality education must be adequately done so that the child will be properly informed. The parent should talk to the child about the changes that will take place in her body so that it will not come as a surprise. When a girl is properly informed about herself, she will not fall a victim of abuse. The sexuality education is also for the boys.

3. Poverty: Some older men can take advantage of poor children and entice them with material things. Exposure to sex from hawking due to molestation

from older men. Some parents also send their children/ward to men to get money for them.

4. Sexual abuse: Rape, deceits, ignorance, etc. Some girls are pregnant because of rape cases that are not reported and medically taken care of.

5. Peer group – exploitation: Due to lack of or inadequate sexuality education, teenagers may exploit themselves by fiddling with parts of their body. This act of exploiting the body with opposite sex can lead to pregnancy. Bad peer group can also deceive someone to sex by saying things like if you are a virgin you develop fibroid, you have pimples all over the body, etc. They will come up with all sorts of lie to make you get into premarital sex.

6. Parents – role and relationship with the child: Parent-child relationship is very important. Parents should have good communication with their children so that when they are abused, they can easily report it without any fear. When there is good communication, the child can tell the parent something that will make the parent sense an intended abuse. For instance if a child tells a parent that some uncle touched my breast and said it is fine, the parent will sense what the uncle is up to and warn the uncle. The parent will also watch the child's friends to keep the child away from bad influences. This is because even if a child is properly trained, once he/she keeps bad company, the child can easily get spoilt by his/her peer group. Parents should allow their children proper freedom of speech for better relationship with them.

7. Promotion of condom instead of absenteeism from sex till marriage: The society now promotes condom in such a way that people abuse it. Abstinence from sex till marriage should be promoted and not condom. Research has proved that condom can fail.

8. Pornography through films, internets, magazines, journals, novels, television series, music, which are wrongly promoted by the media are all killing our youths. Learning from imitation and mimicking licentious behaviour from older adults is another thing that affects young adults. The media promote immorality in a way that young adults see immorality as a way of life. Parents should guide what their children read as well. Watch and listen with them so that you can guide them properly so that they do not get the wrong information about morality. Pornography has played a major role in disseminating information that causes pre-marital sex.

Implications of teenage pregnancy.

1. Inadequate prenatal care which leads to health issues for both the mother and child. Children of older women are healthier than children of young mothers. Older mothers give high quality maternity care than the younger ones. Inadequate nutrition which results in weight loss in babies is common among teenage mothers. Older mothers are better prepared on the task ahead than the teenage mothers.

2. Underdeveloped pelvis can make childbirth difficult which can lead to death in developing nations. In developed nation, caesarean section can be carried

out. Difficulty in childbirth due to underdeveloped pelvis can lead to obstetric fistula, eclampsia, infant or maternal death of either or both.

3. Social stigma: There is a stigma attached to single mothers in the society. They are looked down on.

4. Dropping out of school which of course limits the person's income due to protracted unemployment, low options to job, insecure job, and poorly paid job.

5. Emotional imbalance: Desertion, denial, social stigma, stress in pregnancy etc., can emotionally drain up single mothers.

6. Financial pressure: Raising the child alone can be financially challenging. At the teenage age, the girl will not have source of income and this makes her situation to be difficult.

7. Low self- esteem: The girl may develop low self-esteem due to social stigma and earlier rejection.

8. The child may have developmental disability, low psychosocial development which is caused by the parent's emotional state during pregnancy. Most single parents that had emotional distress when pregnant may give birth to dull and irresponsive child because from conception they feel the rejection and trauma of their mother.

Risk factors in teenage pregnancy.

1. Family issues with regular conflict between members.

2. Violence and sexual abuse in childhood.

3. Unstable housing arrangements.

4. Poor school performance and attendance.

5. Lukewarm attitude towards education partly due to social stigma.

6. Low socioeconomic background.

7. Family history of teenage pregnancies.

8. Discrimination from family members and peer group.

9. Early exposure to emotional distress like rejection, loneliness, and heartbreak.

10. Postnatal depression from teenage mothers due to lack of support, isolation from family and friends, financial pressures, societal attitude, rejection or denial from the father of the child.

11. Lack of antenatal care can lead to miscarriage, premature birth, low birth weight baby due to poor nutrition, birth defects due to drugs, alcohol (foetal alcoholic syndrome), tobacco etc.

12. There is no welfare support from government for single parents in developing countries.

13. Feelings of guilt.

14. Children born to teenage mothers are more vulnerable to neglect and abuse due to poverty, parenting inexperience, or being involved in an unhealthy relationship.

15. Low birth weight babies are more likely to have organs that are not fully developed which can lead to complications such as bleeding in the brain, respiratory distress syndrome, and intestinal problems.

16. Teenage mothers may not tend to take recommended daily multivitamins to maintain adequate nutrition during pregnancy. They are more likely to take drugs, and alcohol which can cause problems such as FAS (Foetal Alcoholic Syndrome).

17. Children born to teenage mothers are less likely to receive proper nutrition, healthcare, cognitive and social stimulation. As a result, they may have an underdeveloped intellect and attain lower academic achievement.

18. Teenage pregnancies are associated with an increased rate of delinquent behaviours in fathers, including alcohol or substance abuse, lower educational level, and reduced earning potential.

b. Marriage Break - Up.

Marriage break – up which could come in the form of divorce, separation, or annulment is the end of a marriage before the death of either of the spouse. Marriage break up can also be as a result of desertion of one of the spouse. Studies have shown that it is the second most stressful event after the death of a spouse.

Effects of marriage break – up.

1. Negative emotional feelings such as deep grief, regret, guilt, depression, anger, anxiety, sadness, lethargy (weariness, sluggishness, tiredness).

2. The cost of divorce like child and spousal support can be financially stressful.

3. Teenage pregnancy, adult prison, truancy in school, juvenile delinquency, school dropout, doing drugs, which are all linked to unemployment, can be a product of broken home.

4. Medical and psychological implications of divorce are chronic diseases such as heart diseases and cancer.

5. Positive effects of divorce on affected children are as follows:

   a) They may be forced to keep their own marriage knowing what they missed growing up in the hand of one parent.

b) For children that experienced domestic violence on their mum, they may learn not to be that way and show affection to their spouse.

c) For children that experience child negligence, they may learn better ways of treating their children knowing what they lacked while growing up.

d) They may decide to take their time in getting married so that it will not break up.

e) They may decide and work out to be better father or mother than their parents knowing the implications of break up.

c. **Adoption.**

Adoption is the legal act of permanently placing a child with a parent or parents other than the biological parents. The order of adoption has the effect of severing parental responsibilities and rights of parents and transferring them to the adoptive parents. After the final process of an adoption, there is no legal difference between the adopted child and biological child.

Infants are more commonly sought for than toddlers or older children because the adoptive parents may want to be the one to build the child the way he, she or they want. Raising infants the way one wants is easier than the toddler or older children who have had some other type of training from other people.

A child should be raised in a secure and loving environment for them to develop well physically, emotionally, and spiritually.

Biological – Custodian} Mordecai adopted Esther. A biological relation may

Guardian} decide to take care of a child if the parents are late/

↗ Tutelage} they cannot take care of the child or is abandoned.

Adoption

↘

Non-biological – The legal process of adopting a child.

Reasons for adoption.

1. Death of both parents of the child. A relation of either parent may decide to adopt the child which may not necessarily need legal process.

2. When the child is dumped and the birth parents cannot be traced.

3. Where the birth parent or parents is available, they decide to place the child on adoption because they cannot carter for the child.

4. Couple that do not have their own children may decide to adopt.

5. Having compassion for adopted children could be a reason for adoption. Someone or a couple may decide to help the children by adopting them even after having their own biological child or children.

6. Some people that have chronic inheritable disease may decide to adopt in order not to transfer the disease through procreation.

7. Unmarried woman who have passed the age of fertility may decide to adopt children. The reason is for the child to keep them company, take care of them when they grow old, share affection, or for the love of children.

8. Religious reasons of helping the afflicted.

d. Surrogacy.

Surrogacy is a method of assisted reproduction whereby a woman agrees to become pregnant for the purpose of gestating and giving birth to a child for others to raise.

A surrogate mother or birth mother is the woman who is pregnant with the child but intends to give it out after birth.

The commissioning parents are the individual that intend to rear the child after birth. Artificial insemination is the process by which sperm is placed into a female's uterus (intrauterine) or cervix (intra cervical) using artificial means rather than by natural sex. The sperm may be from a donor or from the commissioning woman's husband. The aim is to impregnate the woman by non-sexual insertion of sperm into the vagina or uterus.

The bearing of the pregnancy alone is what makes it single parenting because parenting starts from the womb. Most times the surrogate mother does not stay with the commissioning parent(s). In most cases, the surrogate mother will be far from the commissioning parent(s) so that she will not trace them later to start requesting for the child. The surrogate mother is monitored while she carries the baby alone. Some surrogate mothers do this for the money or to help the couple. In some cases, the surrogate mother may be one of the commissioning parents' relations.

e. **Widowhood.**

Widowhood is a state of losing one's spouse to death.

A widow is a woman whose husband has died and a widower is a man whose wife has died.

Effects of widowhood.

All parts of the being is affected during bereavement such as mental, physical, spiritual, emotional, and social well-being of the person.

1. The death of the sole provider of the family can lead to poverty to the home. This happens when it is only one spouse that is working and providing for the family. Women are the most victims of this situation, though men can be a victim of this situation too.

2. Mourning of a spouse can be devastating and can last for a very long time.

3. It can be stressful and lead to depression and death if not properly taken care of.

4. Hardship is experienced because the load of two is carried by one.

5. A future plan can be disrupted or terminated. Hopes and dreams of coming years are shattered which can be heart-breaking.

6. Loneliness: It could be difficult to go to bed and find yourself alone. Issues that were formerly shared will

be hard to decide alone. The role of the other will always be missed and felt.

7. Fear: The bereaved spouse will always feel he or she is seeing or hearing the things that the late spouse used to do such as flipping of paper, shovelling of legs, laughter, moving of chairs, shifting of curtain, opening and closing of doors and windows, hearing voice as if saying something to you, the person's footsteps. These occur because you wish you could feel all that again.

8. Physical exhaustion, uncontrollable crying, sleep disruption, palpitation, shortness of breath, incessant headache, anger, recurrent infections, high blood pressure, loss of appetite, stomach upset, visual and auditory hallucination, worsening of chronic conditions such as asthma.

9. Psychosomatic illness. This is the type of illness that the person feels that something is happening to his/her body such as itching, crawling movement, etc. This illness is not physical; it is rather psychological due to stress.

10. Effects on the nervous system such as lethargy, release of high levels of natural steroids and a heightened state of awareness in the nervous system especially in the autonomic nervous system. The autonomic nervous system is the fight and flight system that controls the body's readiness for action. The heart responds most to this greater nervous drive with an increase in pulse and blood pressure.

11. Decreased immunity: It causes the fall in activity of the T-lymphocytes, cells that are very important in fighting infection, therefore cold and other minor infections are common. Painful problems like rheumatism, arthritis, and other chronic diseases that already exist are worsened. Diabetes and high blood pressure is worsened as well. If the high blood pressure is not controlled, it will lead to stroke.

12. Depression may disrupt sleep and cause loss of appetite.

13. Anxiety which can cause racing pulse, hot sweats, poor sleep, and loss of appetite as well.

14. The bereaved may resort to alcohol and other hard substances that will possibly worsen the person's health condition.

Coping in widowhood.

Life is never the same after losing a spouse but it can still be treasured if properly managed. The grieving in the first year of lose is hard and the grief is very intense.

1. It is good to get in contact with others in widowhood to share sorrow and learn how they have been coping.

2. Do not allow yourself to be lonely when you have friends and relations to interact with.

3. Going on holiday can be very helpful. It is best for you to go somewhere you have not been with your late spouse to avoid having fresh memory of both of

you. Holiday with your children and other people that can lighten up your mode. Holidaying keeps you away from the vicinity that makes you miss your late spouse.

4. Find support group. If you cannot find any, create one with people around or in your church that are in the same condition with you. You can organise a holiday with this group and their family to make it more fun.

5. Read books that deals with coping with widowhood. Articles and journals that are devoted to answering questions on how to cope as a widow or widower can also be of good help.

Remarriage in widowhood.

Some people may choose to stay alone while some others may start seeking for a new relationship. Some others feel guilty building a new relationship. In Africa, widowers usually remarry more than the widows do. Some widows do not always remarry; they prefer to take care of the children except in a situation where the widow is childless. Remarriage is more common with widowers even at a very old age. This is because women cope better in stressful situations than the men.

•   Remarriage may not really be the best option but instead of sleeping around or getting involved in an indecent affair, it is better to get married.

•   Remarriage is not something you have to rush into. You need to remarry for a genuine reason. Take your time to study the person and be sure it's what you want. Getting married to the wrong person does not help you in anyway rather it reminds you of what you miss in your late spouse.

- In starting all over again, make sure your children are aware of it. Get the person you want to get married to, to be close to your children. It may not be easy for the children to accept the person; you need to work on that. Do not say that how your children feels about the person you want to get married to is not necessary. It is very necessary for your children to accept the person for a peaceful home.

- The person you are getting married to must be able to accept your children whole heartedly.

- It is best you live with your children. Both of you should agree on getting the children involved in your relationship. If both of you have children, you can agree to leave together.

- Avoid romantic moves in your children's presence.

- Your children should take precedence in all that you do. The children first, then the intending spouse.

- In courtship, avoid sexual intimacy. Relationship can be as sweet as ever without sexual intercourse. It is a fact that one of the greatest challenges of single parents is sexual desire but one can control his/herself. Self-control means being in control of yourself and not things around you being in control of you.

- Do not think of leave-in mate. In courtship, both of you should leave separately until the wedding. Remember children learn better by examples.

- Get the children involved in the marriage and wedding plans.

Reasons for remarriage.

1. Loneliness.

2. Childlessness.

3. Quest for more children.

4. Quest for male/female child.

5. Need for an assistance.

6. To satisfy sexual desire.

Effects of bereavement on children.

1. Tummy pains, headaches, bed wetting, irritability, insomnia may be experienced by the child or children due to emotional stress.

2. Behavioural problems such as becoming wild, unruly behaviour, being withdrawn, and being sulky.

Response to bereavement.

- Constant medical check-up for both parent and child is very important to monitor the health of both during bereavement.

- In bereavement, the bereaved tends to wear the cloth of the deceased just to have a feel of the person as a result of trying to feel the person.

- The bereaved may decide to burn the cloth he/she was wearing the day the deceased died. This is a way of trying to erase things that will prompt the fresh remembrance of the sad saga.

- Disbelief: At the initial stage of bereavement, the bereaved calls out the name of the deceased to know if the person will answer. This happens because the bereaved have not yet accepted the fact that the deceased is lifeless.

- Men and women grieve alike but women tend to express theirs more.

- Sometimes the bereaved tries to avoid reminders of the deceased.

- Guilt feeling occurs most times such as, "I would have done this or that to save him/her", "I wish I was there, he/she would not have died", "I was a bit careless", etc.

- Confusion may set in.

- In cases such as air crash where the body has to be identified, it is usually disheartening. It is worst when there is no body to mourn.

Answering children's question about death.

Q: What is death?
A: When someone dies, he is lifeless which means no eating, drinking, playing, working, etc. The person cannot do anything.

Q: Will I still see dad/mum again?
A: No, you will not but you have the pictures.

Q: So no dad/mum again to take care of the things mum/dad use to do?
A: God will take care of that. Don't forget that I am there for you anytime any day for anything dad/mum can do for you.

Q: Why should there be death when it is painful?
A: Death is the end of someone's life. Everything that has beginning must have an end. Birth is the beginning of life while death is the end of life.

Q: What is funeral?
A: It is a period when family members, friends, colleagues, relations, neighbours, well-wishers and all that care and know the deceased gather together to pay their last respect to the deceased.

Q: What happens in funeral?
A: People gather for the rite to mourn, sing, and pray for the deceased.

Do not ever avoid any question rather postpone it to get a better answer to the question.

Parent's death in childhood.

The way the surviving parent will attend to the needs of the children will affect the way they cope with bereavement. The loss of a parent is the greatest loss for children. They need support nurturing and continuity.

Parent's death in adulthood.

It is natural and more acceptable for parents to die before their children though it is difficult to come to terms with.

f. Desertion.

Desertion is a form of single parenting whereby a man abandons a woman with children and disappears or a woman abandons a man with the children unexpectedly. In this situation, the reason for abandonment may not be known. The person that is with the child/children is left to parent the child/children alone. To the other party, it is sudden but to the party deserting, it is planned. Desertion can be a ground for divorce in some places after a period of time. It is also a ground for adoption if a child is deserted by the parent or parents. It is a ground for adoption on the basis that there is no one to parent the child. The child will be given out for foster then at a certain age mostly 18 years, he/she can be adopted if the parent/parents do not show up.

g. Distant Marriage.

When couple leave apart, one person is left to parent the children alone. Distant marriage could be **national** when the couple stay apart in the same country. It could be **international** when the couple stay apart in different countries. Most times the reason is to make both ends meet or for some other reason that is usually important to the family. When a man is engaged in a job that keeps him moving from one place to the other, he may decide to leave the wife and children one place and visit once in a while. A man who stays outside the country may come back home to get a wife. One factor or the other may make the wife not to go and stay with the husband. The man may be coming back once in a while to stay with the family. This situation makes the woman to do the parenting alone.

3. Coping with the Difficulties of Single Parenting.

1. Finance: It is cheaper to leave in two than one. Two heads are better than one. Plan on how to use your finance more effectively by investing the money you have in business or stock. If your family refuse to support you financially, start up something no matter how small. Everything big started from something small. Do not be solely dependent on anybody. Bear in mind that you will always cope, and change is constant. Find something doing so that you have a steady source of income. If you were living in a big house before you became a single parent, you can partition your house and rent it out. Someone may be living in a mansion before the situation of single parenting came in, it is better to rent out some part or pack into a cheaper apartment. You can also change the child's school to a cheaper but good one. In all this change, it will be good to carry the children along and explain to them why things are being changed. No matter how little your earning is, save from it. Take out some percentage of your income every month for the school fees, electricity bills, house rent etc. It is also wise to have children's account for the future.

2. Health: Always go for a routine check-up. The doctor needs to confirm that you are alright and sound on regular basis. This is to avoid developing a complicated illness. Health check is good for everyone but it is more vital for young widows and divorcees because of the emotional trauma they go through.

3. Organisation: Planning schedules and sharing duties can be productive. Draw your schedule out from Sunday to Saturday that includes your house chores, social activities, spiritual activities, work schedule, activities for your children etc. This will make you not to be confused on what to do and where to start. You can be writing out activities for the next day, the night before. Time planning makes you to be better organised. Setting limits on the children and on the demands of work by being more assertive may rebalance your life. If you are raising children that go to school and you are also working, you can make different dishes during the weekend that will last throughout the upper week. Ration the dishes in food pack (the size for one person) and store in freezer. In the morning during weekdays, you just have to microwave the packs of food and put in flask for yourself and the children for the day.

4. In cases of loneliness, use your support system – friends, family, colleagues if any, and also seek help from counselling psychologists. You can invite little cousins, nieces, nephews, and family friends over the weekend to assist you in the house chores. Invite another single parent and his/her children and allow them sleep over. The parent you are inviting must be the same sex with you and someone you can trust to

an extent. Develop relationship with adults. Pursue both your children's hobbies and interest and yours as well.

5. Accept your imperfections - be willing to accept ideas, insights, allow yourself to grow and change. Recognize your strengths and do not go beyond your limits.

6. Go for counselling often: Well trained counsellors can be very helpful because they give you strategies in coping as a single parent. Seek help from the internet and share experiences and coping strategies with other single parents.

7. Don't be too independent: Seek helps from new friends if your family and friends reject you. Raise your shoulders high if you are a teenager or a young adult single parent who is being rejected by friends and family. Do not allow the negative things people tell you to get to you, just move on with positivity in your lifestyle.

8. Move on with your normal life. Continue your education if you dropped out because of pregnancy. Work towards achieving your goal in life and make sure you get to where you have always wanted to be. People that reject you will start accepting you back if you start afresh with a responsible life.

9. Learn about children and their different stages of physical, social, cognitive, psychological, and sexual development. This will guide you to understand your children better. Nothing should be strange to you

as a parent in the growth of your children. Get the children involved in appropriate ways.

10. Don't be afraid to start up a new relationship. But this time around, you have to be more careful. Before starting up a relationship, you have to be matured enough for it and get yourself well prepared for it. Your child(ren) may not readily accept your new lover but you have to make them understand why you are involved in the relationship.

4. Growing a Happy Home As a Single Parent.

1. Get along with family and friends. Build up a close relationship with someone good if family and friends are not close by.

2. Take care of the children as much as you can by teaching and training them on the basic things they should know, comforting them, educating them, giving them support, providing them with the basic necessities of life. Meeting with their basic needs, gives you a sense of purpose and makes you happy as a good parent.

3. Enjoy positive emotions. We are more likeable when in positive emotions. Good feeling affects us, the children and the people around.

4. Instil positive behaviour on your children. Always try to be optimistic about them.

5. Always give your children attention. Listen to them when they talk. Be attentive and sensitive to their

emotions. It makes them feel loved. Always give them the right response to their feelings.

6. Allow them express themselves freely with you. The feeling could be talking, crying, yelling, shouting, etc. Find out the reasons for all that and respond to them appropriately.

7. Feel free with your children and you will be surprised to learn new things from them.

8. Go down to their age to learn them more and establish a better relationship with them. Play with them, watch cartoons with them, watch movies with them, and listen to music with them to feel their age. This will remind you of your childhood and make the children to easily open up to you. Participating with them in all these may not be fun or easy to cope with but you just need to be that "childish" sometimes to move along with them.

9. Try to exert discipline to your child when necessary without feeling guilty.

10. Avoid labelling: Anger can make you call your child undesirable names. Remember that your child is what you call him/her. Try to calm down when the child upsets you. It is not necessary to call your children names when they get you upset.

11. Use your life situation to teach your child or children so that they will be able to tackle difficulties that may come their way in future. You are your child's greatest teacher, live an exemplary life. Avoid bringing

in different men that are not relations into the house. Children learn by imitation. Parents are children's first role model. Be mindful of your actions because they follow your footsteps.

12. You can send your child to your brother or sister that stays with the spouse once in a while so that the child will have the feel of staying where both parents are living together. This will go a long way in helping him/her psychologically.

13. Learn to do things together like cooking, baking, washing, playing, exercising, gardening, decorating and tidying up of the house. Do the best you can to keep the family together and afloat.

14. Create a conducive home for yourself and the children where you all can relate appropriately. Make the home as comfortable as you can by keeping it tidy and fresh all the time.

15. Availability is the most important aspect of parenting. Parenting is not just about providing and protecting, it is more about being there when you are needed.

16. Do not allow other people give your children first-hand information about them. In cases where the child or children is a love child, adopted or the child is through surrogacy, you should be the first to tell the child about it. Do not be afraid of losing the child. A responsible child will appreciate you more. That is why it is important to raise your child responsibly enough. Tell them the story behind their birth or adoption. The age to telling this matters as they have to be matured

enough to take it. It is not wise to hide a child's history to him or her. You can tell who the father is and where he is from to avoid the child going through the trauma of searching for the father. I suggest age 18 though it could be earlier than that if the child is maturing fast.

17. Encourage your children to regard their family situation as normal. Let them not feel that they are different from other children that stay with both parents. Point it out to them that they are like them and could be better than them.

18. Be open to your children. Be their best friend. Share your daily work experience with them, that way they can open up and share their daily school activities as well. When they do not open up to share their activities in school, you can ask questions that will prompt them to open up. Build good communication with them. Make them understand that you will always stand by them at all times.

19. You can get a father – figure or a mother – figure for them. The father or mother figure will best be your parents, siblings or other trust worthy close relation.

20. If you are divorced or separated, make visiting arrangement with the other parent. They deserve to know their biological father or mother and spend some good time with them. It affects children psychologically when they keep imagining who the parent is and what their father or mother is like. The visiting of the other parent should be scheduled to be regular.

5. How to Handle the Stress of Single Parenting.

The work load in single parenting is more when the child has chronic medical problem, mental health issue, behavioural problems, learning disabilities, and have some emotional problems. It could be very stressful and painful to carry the load alone. Meeting up with the demands of the child and still take care of yourself and go to work is not an easy task. Single parenting in such situation is usually different and more tasking from regular parenting because the single parent bears the pain alone.

1. Try to see every hard situation as a very positive one. Try to find and appreciate the positive side of difficult situations.

2. Know your limit in doing anything and everything. Do not exceed your limit.

3. Eat three square meals daily but if the finance is too hard make it breakfast and dinner. Legumes, fruits, and vegetables are very essential for your health.

4. Have enough sleep of nothing less than seven hours at night.

5. Exercise regularly for at least once a week. Exercise makes one to be more active. From my own experience, exercise reduces my pain threshold. It makes you happy and more active. Exercise and eat properly in order to keep fit and to ease off tension

6. Give yourself a good treat. Take a warm bath, get your meal delivered, and go for beauty treatment if you can afford them.

7. Enjoy yourself by attending social events, going for cinemas, visiting the beach etc. In all of this, your children must be involved.

8. Enumerate stressors around you and create ways of handling them.

9. If you have a child with special needs, you can employ someone to be assisting the child especially when you are working. If you cannot afford this, get a relation that is not yet employed to assist you. You can also take the child to boarding school to be visiting on weekends and the child can always come back during holidays. If you are financially balanced, you can reduce your work hour to spend more time with the child. Make sure the child does not miss his/her appointment with the health expert that is handling him/her. In everything, don't forget that your unconditional love and care to the child can do more healing than what medicine can do.

6. How to Be a Successful Single Parent.

1. Organisation: You have to be well organised. Prov 21:5, "The plans of the diligent lead to profit as surely as haste leads to poverty."

2. Take your family as priority. Place your family first before anything – 1 Tim 5:8.

3. Tackle your challenges diligently and find creative ways of coping with difficulties.

4. Good method of communication is very important. Openly and politely express your feelings and thoughts to your family. Gather your children and discuss family issues with them. You can discuss an important issue over a dinner.

5. Wine and dine with your family always in odd times and good times.

6. Try to control your negative emotions so that it does not affect the child.

7. You do not need to be tattered. You need to take good care of yourself and provide for your needs as well.

8. Look at the positive side of single parenting like freedom to do things on your own without interruption and do not cling to the negative aspect of it.

9. Bible study can be helpful. Create interesting ways of studying the bible not alone but with your child.

10. Pray always and pray together with your child. A family that prays together stays together.

11. Keep up with your dreams. Take time to make a schedule of what you intend to accomplish in life and take your time to work towards achieving them. Do not allow your dreams to die.

12. Visit other people in need such as the elderly, sick, handicapped so that you can appreciate your own condition.

13. Avoid alcohol and other hard substance, overeating, oversleeping, and smoking because they do not help rather they worsen your personal health thereby creating more problems for you.

14. You can turn your feeling of loneliness into a creative poem or story and send it out for competition. You can as well publish the story or poem and make money from it. You can also write a song or launch an album written from your feelings. Winning a competition and/or making money from the album, poem, or story

will make you appreciate your condition and see the better side of yourself and your condition.

15. Always be optimistic in all that you do. Always see the good side of your situation. Occupying your mind with regrets and guilt feelings will make you to feel worst and will not allow you to discover the best of you. As a single parent you can easily make decisions without permission from anyone. You are more self-reliant, independent, and responsible than your counterparts.

16. Have a motivating and encouraging write-ups pasted close to your bed-side, kitchen, restroom, and other corners of the house. It could be bible quotations or inspirational quotes from people.

17. Always have at the back of your mind that time heals all wounds and that no condition is permanent.

18. You have to be hard working to achieve your goals in life. Put extra effort to craft out the best in you.

7. Handling Single Mother Pregnancy.

Factors that lead to single mother pregnancy are as follows:

1. Teenage pregnancy.

2. An unplanned pregnancy as a result of pre-marital sex.

3. Surrogacy.

4. Death of the father of the child.

5. Denial and abandonment of the father of the child.

6. Unknown pregnancy that occurs just before a break-up.

How to cope with pregnancy as a single mother.

1. Go for antenatal and keep to hospital appointments.

2. Take multivitamin tablets that will help the growth of the child and will protect against miscarriage.

Examples of such vitamins are folic acid, vitamin A and B, etc. Whatever drug you are taking must be under doctor's prescription. Avoid self-medication, it endangers your life.

3. Be consoled that some women have been pregnant and raised their children alone.

4. Feed well with fruit, vegetables, enough water, grains, legumes, etc.

5. Relax and have enough sleep. Find an orchard or garden where you can go and lye with your mat to receive fresh air. While lying and relaxing, close your eyes and fantasize on sweet things. Think about how beautiful the child will be and other positivity of being a mother. This will relax your mind, body, and soul.

6. Avoid stressful situations.

7. As you are pregnant, pray and talk to your baby. Grooming starts from the womb. Touch your tummy and pray to God that your baby does not inherit the negative side of you and the father. Tell God what you want the child to be in future. Pray that the baby inherits the positive side of you and the father. You will be surprise that all you tell God about your baby will manifest when the baby comes out.

8. Pamper yourself and love your body. Soak yourself in a bath tub filled with good smelling shower gel and listen to music of your choice while being soak there. Always feel cool. Take good care of yourself and always appear neat and clean.

9. Love yourself, your baby, your condition, and see yourself as blessed.

10. Get your own personal doctor or midwife to check you up and tell how you feel at all times. The professionals will assist in answering questions that are stocked in your mind about pregnancy. Get acquainted to them, in that way you may not need to pay for consultation.

11. Get a diary or book where you will be recording what happens in your body at any given time. Go to antenatal with it and show your doctor. If you feel something severe, call the doctor over the phone and book an appointment immediately.

12. Don't ever see the child as a mistake but as a bundle of joy and blessing.

13. Do not fail to do exercise. Brisk walk of thirty minutes can do. The doctor can tell better.

14. Pick pregnancy book, birth book, and other books on how to groom children. The books will help you get yourself prepared for the coming of the child.

15. You can also watch birth stories. Watch the positive ones that will not make you get scared of delivery.

Getting prepared for delivery.

1. Buy baby things ahead of time. If you cannot afford them, do not be shy to ask close relatives to lend or give you theirs.

2. Get your bag ready for the appointed day ahead of time. This will help you to just pick it up and go to hospital in case labour should start at any time. You do not need to start arranging your things in the bag when labour comes.

3. Get the phone close to you in case labour should come at any time so that you can call the ambulance or call someone that will be available to rush you to the hospital.

4. You can get a relation to stay with you while the date approaches. You can as well go and stay with family members to be on the safe side.

5. Cook enough food in advance and store in freezer so that you have enough to eat when you come back from hospital.

6. Look out for doting friends and relations that can accompany you to the labour room so that you do not feel the pain alone.

7. You can arrange for a baby sitter ahead of time if you can afford it. If you cannot afford to pay a baby sitter, you can beg a relation to come and stay with you. Preferably, go and stay with family members if they do not mind.

8. Parent - Child Bonding.

Parental bonding is the process of affectionate attachment that parents develops for a child. From the time the baby is in the womb to the time the baby is being delivered, the parent should be emotionally attached to the baby by touching the tummy and saying nice things to the unborn child. Most psychologists believe that the training of the child starts from the womb which is right. You can say nice things such as: 'I can't wait to have you', 'mum loves you', 'you are a special gift from God', etc. When the baby kicks, you can ask the baby, is there anything you want?, should I change my position? What is it baby? You can also tell the baby, 'please stop kicking it hurts' or 'please keep calm mum needs rest', etc. A good number of mothers feel the baby's response when they talk to them. Immediately after delivery, the baby is handed over to the mother for them to have the first warmth together – bonding. This bonding goes a long way to affect the child's development in future. Babies who feel the acceptance of their mum from womb socialize better than babies that are rejected.

Maternal bonding is said to be one of the strongest type of bonding. The hormone oxytocin which pregnant and nursing mothers produce reduces anxiety and in a way fosters bonding. This is to show that nature has a way of instilling and nurturing bonding between parent and child.

For a parent that adopts, it could take them a while to start the bonding. For such people they should start preparing and learning ways to bond before the arrival of the baby. This will make bonding faster and easier than waiting to start to think of it when the baby is already at hand.

In a situation where a woman dies in child birth, paternal bonding should take place immediately. The mother doesn't necessarily need to die for paternal bonding to occur. Father's best way of bonding is by playing with the child. In this situation, the father should also get himself more involved with the baby by bottle feeding the baby himself. During bottle feeding, the father should try and have constant eye contact with the baby. The father should learn other ways of bonding with the baby.

The aim of bonding is to build good interpersonal relationship between parent and child. It makes both the parent and child happy. It makes the parent to feel responsible and the child to feel loved and cared for. Bonding gives the child sense of security and confidence.

Ways of bonding.

1. Breast feeding – Breast feeding is a way of bonding the baby and mother. It is said that most people are closer to their mum because of the eye contact they share during breast feeding. Breast feeding is a very good way of studying the baby's body language. The feel of

being nourished by the mother gives the baby a sense of well-being. Waking up at the middle of the night to feed your baby with just the two of you awake makes both of you feel special love for each other. This is the best way of bonding.

2. Play with the baby. Both of you can play with toys as well.

3. Baby massage – It calms the baby, helps the baby to wind when the back is being massaged. Massaging relaxes the baby and makes him/her to sleep. Touching is a good way of showing the baby how much you appreciate him/her.

4. Bath-time – This is a good time of bonding with the baby. Moving the baby through the water. Tickle the baby while bathing him/her. You can as well bath together with the baby to have a good feel of you.

5. Backing the baby is a way of having good body contact with the baby. It gives the baby sense of security.

6. Singing – Singing to the baby is another way. You must not be a good singer to sing to your baby. It gives the baby joy to hear your voice. If you observe you will see that the baby feels happy hearing your voice.

7. Story time – Create time for telling your child story. Even though the baby is yet to understand, do not be surprise that you are conveying a message that will linger and impact positively on your child. As the baby grows, share story books with him/her.

8. Changing the diaper – Gently remove the stained diaper. Clean the baby up. Rub in powder or petroleum jelly on the baby's buttocks and around his buttock in a way that will make him feel relaxed. Then after you can replace the diaper with a new one. This gentle process shows the baby how much you care.

9. Communicate with your baby in any manner you wish. Just vocalise as the baby does. If the baby is cooing, coo with him/her. If he/she is babbling, just follow suit. You can also communicate with a sign language. Just flow with your baby in a way that both of you understand each other.

10. Sleeping in the same room with your baby – You can have the baby's cot close to your bed. Sleeping in the same bed can be risky to avoid SIDS – Sudden Infant Death Syndrome. Responding to the baby's movement and other stimulation is a good way of bonding with the baby.

11. Feel the baby all the time through frequent cuddling and touching.

Spending quality time with your child.

1. You can start up small business that involves them. Get them involved in your other plans as well.

2. Do gardening with them.

3. Play games with them. Complete puzzle, crafts, and other projects for them, play hide and seek with them, etc.

4. Visit museum, parks, malls, zoos and other interesting places with them.

5. Volunteer to help them especially the handicapped.

6. Assist in their take home assignment but do not do the work for them.

7. You can explore with them by visiting beaches, biking, swimming, fishing, etc.

8. Share meals, videos, movies, sports, and other entertainment with them.

9. Meet with your child's friends. Invite them over to the house. Get to know the family. This will help you to know the type of influence they will have on your child.

10. Meet with your child's teacher as well. Ask about your child's performance and comportment in school. This will help you monitor how your child performs.

11. The last two points make the parent get closer to the child and to understand the child better. It also improves the relationship of the parent and child.

12. Read out stories from story books and children's bible for them and share the story lesson with them.

13. Always tell and show your children that you love and care for them.

14. Avoid discussing the other parent in a negative way with your child.

15. No one can be a better parent to your children than you. Effective parenting needs sacrifices. You have to sacrifice quality time to spend with the child. For instance, belonging to social clubs that will tie you down during weekends when you are supposed to be with your children is not necessary. Belonging to such time consuming social club is only necessary when the children are grown and are not always around. It is better to go out with the children to catch fun than leaving them at home to catch up with some other person or people.

16. You have to be a good parent to have good children. Love yourself so that you can love your children. One cannot give what he/she does not have.

Factors that may affect bonding.

1. The hormones such as vasopressin and oxytocin that facilitate bonding may be affected through postpartum depression.

2. In cases of adoption, if the parent has a mental picture of what the baby should be like and it turns out not to be like that, then bonding will be affected.

3. If a mother goes through a prolonged labour or painful delivery, she may be exhausted to bond with the child immediately.

4. Taking drug during delivery may cause drowsiness thereby making the mother not to easily respond to the baby's stimulation.

5. If a baby is placed in an intensive care unit after delivery, bonding may be delayed.

6. Bonding with a baby with health problem can be a bit difficult for the mother.

7. Rejection – When a woman does not accept her pregnancy, it emotionally affect the mother and child. Bonding in a situation of rejection is rare as acceptance is important for bonding.

Effects of bonding.

1. A bonded child socialises better than an un-bonded child.

2. Breastfeeding which is a way of bonding has been found to improve the neurological and cognitive development of a child.

3. Bonded babies are said to be more alert and responsive, and also brighter and healthier.

4. Bonded babies have better self-esteem than the un-bonded one.

5. Lack of bonding can cause inferiority complex later in life as a result of rejection from the parent. This may likely occur in teenage pregnancy.

6. Social deviance and some psychiatric disorder have been linked to lack of parental bonding.

7. A child that lacks bonding may give up to flirting as a result of searching for a father-figure or mother-figure.

8. A bonded child grows to have high self-esteem because he/she grew up with love and care. This high self-esteem is as a result of acceptance and affection found from the parent.

9. A child may grow up to be isolated when there is no bond from anyone including parent, family members, and neighbours.

10. Lack of bonding leads to poor well-being and behavioural disorder in adolescent.

11. Infants that lack bonding tend to be more demanding, insatiable, and irritable which as a result leads to crying all the time. Crying is meant to draw attention of the caregiver but when it is not responded to, the infant tends to be very irritable.

9. How to Raise Your Child to Be Responsible from Childhood.

1. Young children always want to do one thing or the other, encourage them when they seek to do some chores no matter how young the child is. You can encourage them by telling them to replace something, take something from one place to the other, pick up something and drop in the appropriate place, etc.

2. Allow the children around you when you cook, bake, fry, do the laundry, wash dishes and clothes, that way, they will learn how to do those chores themselves. In the course of working you can make them assist by telling them to help rinse the plate while I do the washing, assist me roll the dough, get the soap, open the tap etc.

3. Little chores can be shared to them within the week. Mondays can be one person to assist in washing dishes while the others watch and learn from his/ her mistakes. The other day could be for the other to clean the house, etc. One of them can be cleaning the house while the other dresses the bed. In sending them on little errand, avoid chores that are risky for

children for instance, things that should be kept out of the reach of children, breakable dishes, chemicals of all sorts. Whatever they do must be done under the supervision of an adult.

4. Allow them choose chores for themselves so that they do not do it with annoyance or find the chore tiresome.

5. Make their chores look very unserious by making it fun. One of the ways of doing this is by making them do it as role playing.

6. You should point out to them that assisting in the house chores makes them more responsible children. It also makes them not to be dependent on any one when they grow up.

7. There should be reward for a job well done. The reward could be either having an extra biscuits or chocolates, an outing to a place where he/she likes to visit, buying of gifts etc.

8. There should also be punishment for the non-compliant child. The punishment could be denying the child from playing games or watching television especially his/her favourite programme, he/she could be asked to stay back while others go on outing, buying things for others without giving him especially what he/she likes to eat most.

9. Reward and punishment must always follow the action that attracts it immediately. This will make the child

to associate the reward or punishment with the action that attracted it.

10. Recognise their effort at all times even if it is not properly done. Understand their limits as a child and encourage them by praising them.

10. Ways to Raise Your Children Not to Be Wayward.

1. Give them love and care. Be affectionate to them no matter how odd the circumstances may be. Show them the love and care you feel for them but do not over pamper them. Be strict when necessary and lenient if need be. Do not be afraid of them seeing you as a bad parent if you are sure of doing the right thing at the right time. When the children grow up, they will appreciate the strict times because those times makes them better people in future.

2. You need to be there all the time so that they do not become promiscuous by looking out for father-figure or mother-figure outside.

3. Send them to good school that have good morale.

4. Check their school bag daily to make sure they do not bring in what does not belong to them. If you see something you did not buy with them, investigate on how they got it.

5. Checkmate their every move but not policing them. Do it in such a way that they will not notice. Just be conscious of their every move.

6. Pray for them and make them pray for you as well. Pray to God to give you the wisdom to train the children appropriately.

7. Read the bible with them and share the passage's lesson with them.

8. If they come back home with bruises and wound, find out the cause. Go to school and investigate the matter.

9. Share their emotion with them. Be sensitive to their emotions and react to them appropriately.

10. Choose toys that will help their intellectual ability – such as puzzle, crossword, chase, etc.

11. Teach them the word of God. Teach them to fear God.

12. As a good parent, you must have control over your children and this can only come when you teach your children how to respect you and people that are older than them.

13. Bear in mind that training does not come by force. It takes time and it is a gradual process. You have to be consistent in your manner of training. Changing hand will get them confused.

14. If you have more than one child, make sure that you give them equal love. Don't show that you prefer this person to the other. This will prompt jealousy and dislike which is not healthy for your home. You do not need to have a special child.

15. When disciplining your children, try to control your emotions when they cry. Crying is a sign of remorse and regret. Crying does not kill a child, rather it corrects.

11. How Single Parenting Affects Children.

1. Children of single parents are very likely to share more household responsibilities.

2. Single parents often discuss things with their children because they are the only companion they have. In order words, single parents are well attached to their children.

3. Some of the children tend to be nuisance if they are pampered or they are not well taken care of.

4. Lack of attention (care and love) may make the children to keep bad company in the quest of needing company. It can make the child to be promiscuous while seeking for love and care.

5. In a situation where the child is not appreciated especially in cases of teenage pregnancy, the child may grow to have low self-esteem.

6. Single parent children are more likely to develop self-reliance faster than their peers.

7. So many negative attitudes have been attributed to single parent children whom I researched on and some of these negative hypotheses were refuted. I took a research on 2009 in Nigeria to investigate how single parenting affects the academic performance and self-esteem of the children. I compared the academic performance and self-esteem of children living with single parent and that of children living with both parents and the there was no significant difference. The factors that led to this are high socio-economic status of parent; enabling environment for learning; family support. An important factor is having a mother-figure at home when there is single father and a father-figure at home when there is single mother. Most times the single parent lives with their parents or married sibling which aids her parenting. The single parent child that has the support of the family around and a parent that is well paid, does not have difference with mates in both parent home. Single parenting has negative effect if you decide to parent alone without making use of the people around you.

8. Children from broken home usually feel challenged and work toward having an intact home.

Factors that influence how children develop in single parent families include the following:

1. Parent's age: The more matured the parents, the more they are likely to handle the child.

2. Educational level: Educated people are more likely to have a lucrative job. This makes them to be able to

handle financial issues. Educated people are also likely to be more informed on how to parent.

3. Occupation: Employment gives one steady income. A parent that is employed will cater better for the child than the one that depends on people for livelihood.

4. Family's income: When the family income is large, the parent may not have problem taking care of the child.

5. Family's support network of friends and extended family members including that of the absent parent if available goes a very long way to impact knowledge and sense of well-being to the child.

12. Words of God to Single Parents and Their Children.

Adoption.

∞ Esther was raised by her cousin Mordecai and she was instrumental to the saving of the Jews. Esther 2: 15.

∞ Pharaoh's daughter adopted Moses. Moses delivered his people. Ex 2: 1-10.

∞ God's love for adoptees. – James 1:27 "Religion that God our Father accepts as pure and faultless is this: to look after orphans and widows in their distress and to keep oneself from being polluted by the world."

∞ God adopts us all. – Gal 4:7 "So you are no longer a slave, but a son; and since you are a son, God has made you also an heir." – Rom 8:15 "For you did not receive a spirit that makes you a slave again to fear, but you receive the spirit of sonship (adoption). And by Him we cry Abba Father." – Romans 8: 23 "Not only so, but we ourselves, who have the firstfruits of the spirit, groan inwardly as we wait eagerly for our adoption as sons, the redemption of our bodies."

Bereavement.

∞ God's love and understanding for the broken hearted. – Ps 147:3 "He heals the broken hearted and binds up their wounds." – Jn 14: 1 "Do not let your heart be troubled. Trust in God; trust also in me (Jesus Christ)."

∞ Hope for meeting the dead in future. – 1 Cor 15: 51-52 "Listen, I tell you a mystery: We will not all sleep, but we all be changed – in a flash, in the twinkling of an eye, at the last trumpet. For the trumpet will sound, the dead will be raised imperishable and we will be changed."

∞ God restores Joy. – Is 51: 11 "The ransomed of the Lord will return. They will enter Zion with singing; everlasting joy will crown their heads. Gladness and Joy will overtake them, and sorrow and sighing will flee away."

Loneliness.

∞ Turning to God when lonely. – Ps 23: 4 "Even though I walk through the valley of the shadow of the death, I fear no evil, for you are with me: Your rod and your staff, they comfort me" – Ps 25: 16 "Turn to me and be gracious to me, for I am lonely and afflicted." – Ps 142: 1-4 "I cry aloud to the Lord; I lift up my voice to the Lord for mercy. I pour out my complaint before him; before him I tell my trouble. When my spirit grows where I walk men have hidden a snare for me. I have no refuge; no-one cares for my life."

∞ God encourages the lonely. – Deut 31: 6 "Be strong and courageous. Do not be afraid or terrified because of them, for the Lord your God goes with you; he will never leave you nor forsake you." – Ps 62: 1-2 "My soul finds rest in God alone; my salvation; he is my fortress, I shall never be shaken."

Financial worry.

∞ Heb 13: 5 "Keep your lives free from love of money and be content with what you have, because God has said, 'Never will I leave you; never will I forsake you'." – Jer 29: 11 "For I know the plans I have for you," declares the Lord, "plans to prosper you and not to harm you, plans to give you hope and a future.

Lust.

∞ Nursing lust in mind. – Mt 5: 8 "Blessed are the pure in heart, for they will see God." – James 1: 14-15 "... but each one is tempted when, by his own evil desire, he is dragged away and enticed. Then, after desire has conceived, it gives birth to son; and sin, when it is full-grown, gives birth to death." – I Thess 4: 3-5 "It is God's will that you should be sanctified: that you should avoid sexual immorality; that each of you should learn to control his own body in a way that is holy and honourable, not in passionate lust like the heathen, who do not know God." – 1 Pet 2: 11 "Dear friends, I urge you, as aliens and strangers in the world, to abstain from sinful desires, which war against your soul."

∞ Lust comes as a result of disobedience to the word of God. – Prov 9: 10 "The fear of the Lord is the beginning of wisdom, and knowledge of the Holy one is understanding." – Eph 4: 22-24 "You were taught, with regard to your former way of life, to put off your old self, which is being corrupted by its deceitful desires; to be made new in the attitude of your minds; and to put on the new self, created to be like God in true righteousness and holiness."

∞ You have control over your body and not your body having control over you. – 2 Tim 2: 22 "Flee the evil desires of youth, and pursue righteous, faith, love and peace, along with those who call on the Lord out of a pure heart." – Tit 2: 12 "It teaches us to say 'No' to ungodliness and worldly passions, and to live self-controlled, upright and godly lives in this present age,..." – I Cor 10: 13 "No temptation has seized you except what is common to man. And God is faithful; he will not let you be tempted, he will also provide a way out so that you stand up under it."

Being the responsible parent God wants you to be.

∞ Is 40: 11 "He tends his flock like a shepherd: He gathers the lambs in his arms and carries them close to his heart; he gently leads those that have young."

∞ Is 49: 15 "Can a mother forget the baby at her breast and have no compassion on the child she has borne?..."

∞ Tit 2: 3-5 "Likewise, teach the older women to be revered in the way they live, not to be slanders or addicted to much wine, but to teach what is good.

Then they can train the younger women to love their husbands and children, to be self-controlled and pure, to be busy at home, to be kind,..."

Worries.

∞ Phil 4: 6 "Do not be anxious about anything but in everything, by prayer and petition, with thanksgiving present your requests to God."

∞ Mt 6: 25-34 "Therefore I tell you, do not worry about your life, what you will eat or drink, or about your body, what you will wear. Is not life more important than clothes? Look at the birds of the air, they do not sow or reap or store away in barns, and yet your heavenly Father feeds them. Are you not much more valuable than they? Who of you by worrying can add a single hour to your life? And why do you worry about clothes? See how the lilies of the field grow. They do not labour or spin. Yet I tell you that not even Solomon in all his splendour was dressed like one of these. If that is how God clothes the grass of the field, which is here today and tomorrow is thrown into the fire, will he not much more clothe you, O you of little faith? So do you not worry, saying, 'What shall we eat?' or 'What shall we drink' or 'What shall we wear?' For the pagans run after these things, and your heavenly Father knows that you need them. But seek first his kingdom and his righteousness, and all these things will be given to you as well. Therefore do not worry about tomorrow, for tomorrow will worry about itself. Each day has enough trouble of its own."

∞ Mt 11: 28 "Come to me, all you who are weary and burdened, and I will give you rest."

Being contented (Accept yourself the way you are and appreciate yourself).

∞ Ps 139: 13-14 "For you created my inmost being; you knit me together in my mother's womb. I praise you because I am fearfully and wonderfully made; your works are wonderful, I know that full well."

∞ Phil 4: 12-13 "I know what it is to be in need, and I know what it is to have plenty. I have learned the secret of being content in any and every situation, whether well fed or hungry, whether living in plenty or in want."

∞ Phil 4: 11 "I am not saying this because I am in need, for I have learned to be content whatever the circumstance."

Raising children in the way of God.

∞ Train the child from the womb to fear God. – Ps 58: 3 "Even from birth the wicked go astray, from the womb they are wayward and speak lies."

∞ Deut 6: 6-7 "These commandments that I give you today are to be upon your hearts. Impress them on your children. Talk about them when you sit at him and when you sit at home and when you walk along the road, when you lie down and when you get up – Teach the children the commandments of God at all times and in different situations."

∞ Is 54: 13 "All your sons will be taught by the Lord; and great will be your children's peace – Do your best in training the children the way of God and leave the rest for God."

∞ Prov 29: 15 "The rod of correction imparts wisdom, but a child left to himself disgraces his mother."

∞ Prov 22: 6 "Train a child in the way he should go, and when he is old he will not turn from it."

∞ Ps 34: 11 "Come my children, listen to me, I will teach the fear of the Lord."

∞ Heb 12: 11 "No discipline seems pleasant at the time, but painful. Later on, however, it produces a harvest of righteousness and peace for those who have been trained by it."

∞ 2 Tim 3: 15 "...and how from infancy you have known the Holy Scriptures, which are able to make you wise for salvation through faith in Christ Jesus."

∞ Do not anger your children. – Eph 6: 4 "Fathers, do not exasperate your children; instead, bring them up in the training and instruction of the Lord." – Col 3: 21 "Fathers, do not embitter your children, or they will become discouraged."

Words of God for children.

∞ Prov 1: 8/ Prov 6: 20 "Listen, my son, to your father's instruction and do not forsake your father's teaching."

∞ Eph 6: 1-3 "Children, obey your parents in the Lord, for this is right. "Honour your father and mother" – which is the first commandment with a promise – " that it may go well with you and that you may enjoy long life on the earth."

∞ Col 3: 20 "Children, obey your parents in everything, for this pleases the Lord."

∞ 1 Pet 1: 14-16 "As obedient children, do not conform to the evil desires you had when you lived in ignorance. But just as he who called you is holy, so be holy in all you do; for it is written: "Be holy, because I am holy.""

Widows (Widowers).

∞ Story of widows in the Holy Bible. – Naomi and Ruth (Book of Ruth). – Widow of Zarephath (1 King 17: 7-24). – Widow with two (Mk 12: 41-44). Widow of Nain (Lk 7: 11-15).

∞ God cares for the widow/widowers. – Prov 15: 24 "The Lord tears down the proud man's house but keeps the widows boundaries intact." – Is 46: 4 "Even to your old age and grey hairs I am he, I am he who will sustain you. I have made you and I will carry you; I will sustain you and I will rescue you." – Ps 146: 9 "The Lord watches over the alien and sustains the fatherless and the widow, but he frustrates the ways of the wicked." – Jer 49: 11 "Leave your orphans; I will protect their lives. Your widow too can trust in me."

∞ God's special love for the widows/widowers. – Jer 22: 3 "This is what the Lord says: Do what is just and right.

Rescue from the hand of his oppressor the one who has been robbed. Do no wrong or violence to the alien, the fatherless or the widow, and do not shed innocent blood in this place." – Ex 22: 22-24 "Do not take advantage of a widow or an orphan. If you do and they cry out to me, I will certainly hear their cry." – Deut 10: 18 "He defends the cause of the fatherless and the widow, and loves the alien, giving him food and clothing." – Ps 68: 5 "A father to the fatherless, a defender of widows, is God in his holy dwelling." – Is 54: 5 "For your maker is your husband – the Lord Almighty is his name – the Holy one of Israel is your Redeemer, he is called the God of all the earth." – Zech 7: 10 "Do not oppress the widow or fatherless, the alien or the poor. In your hearts do not think evil of each other."

About the Author.

The author is a marriage instructor who has obtained a bachelor's and master's degree in psychology. She has special interest in counselling and psychotherapy and is training to obtain her doctorate in the field. She is a motivational speaker and is an author of other Christian inspirational books. She is happily married to Charles Azuka Ubah.